LET'S-READ-AND-FIND-OUT SCIENCE®

STAGE 1

What's It Like to Be a Fish?

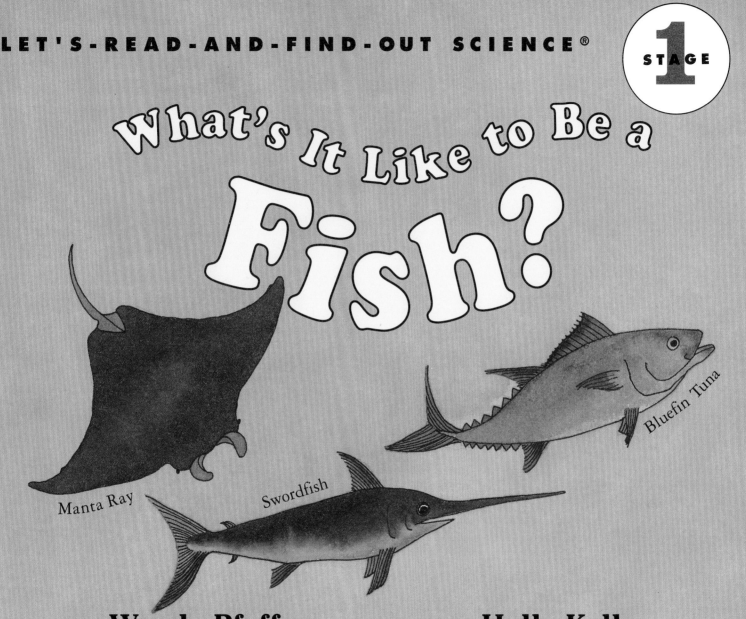

Manta Ray

Swordfish

Bluefin Tuna

by **Wendy Pfeffer**   illustrated by **Holly Keller**

HarperCollinsPublishers

For Tom — W. P.
For Suzanne — H. K.

With sincere thanks to Nancy Siscoe, for her expert guidance; Valerie Chase from the National Aquarium in Baltimore, and Raymond Klinger and Ernest Tresselt at Huntington Creek fisheries, all of whom checked this manuscript for accuracy; Renee Cho, the Wednesday Workshoppers, and my family for their support.
—W.P.

The illustrations in this book were created with pen and ink, watercolors, and pastels
on Rives BFK paper.

Note: The fish pictured on the jacket are a Common Goldfish, Guppies, and Neon Tetras.

The *Let's-Read-and-Find-Out Science* series was originated by Dr. Franklyn M. Branley, Astronomer Emeritus and former Chairman of the American Museum–Hayden Planetarium, and was formerly co-edited by him and Dr. Roma Gans, Professor Emeritus of Childhood Education, Teachers College, Columbia University. Text and illustrations for each of the books in the series are checked for accuracy by an expert in the relevant field. For a complete catalog of Let's-Read-and-Find-Out Science books, write to HarperCollins Children's Books, 10 East 53rd Street, New York, NY 10022.

Library of Congress Cataloging-in-Publication Data
Pfeffer, Wendy, date
    What's it like to be a fish? / by Wendy Pfeffer ; illustrated by Holly Keller.
      p.   cm. — (Let's-read-and-find-out science. Stage 1)
    ISBN 0-06-024428-3. — ISBN 0-06-024429-1 (lib. bdg.) — 0-06-445151-8 (pbk.)
    1. Fishes—Juvenile literature. [1. Fishes.] I. Keller, Holly, ill.   II. Title.   III. Series.
QL617.2.P44 1996   94-6543
597—dc20   CIP
                                                                                                          AC

Typography by Christine Hoffman Casarsa
10 9 8 7 6 5 4 3 2 1
❖
First Edition

What's It Like to Be a Fish?

Calico Goldfish

Veiltail Goldfish

Common Shiners

Lake Whitefish

Smallmouth Buffalo

4

Coho Salmon

Grass Pickerel

Lake Whitefish

Fish live in water—in lakes, ponds,

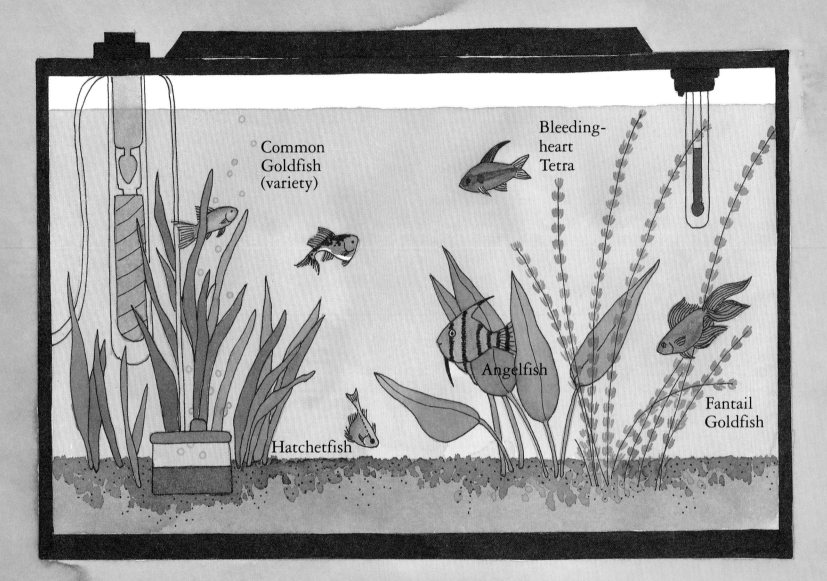

Common
Goldfish
(variety)

Bleeding-
heart
Tetra

Angelfish

Hatchetfish

Fantail
Goldfish

aquariums,

and even plastic bags.

Common Goldfish

Common Goldfish

Your pet goldfish can live in a bowl. You can watch the golden fish slip over and under the castle, hide among the water plants, and glide quietly around in their underwater world.

Calico Goldfish

Common Goldfish (variety)

A fish's body is just right for living underwater, just as your body is right for living on land.

You can swim, but a fish can swim better! A fish's sleek body is the perfect shape for swimming. Fins stick out from the fish's body. They help the fish to swim. A goldfish's tail fin pushes it through the water. Six other fins steady, steer, or stop it.

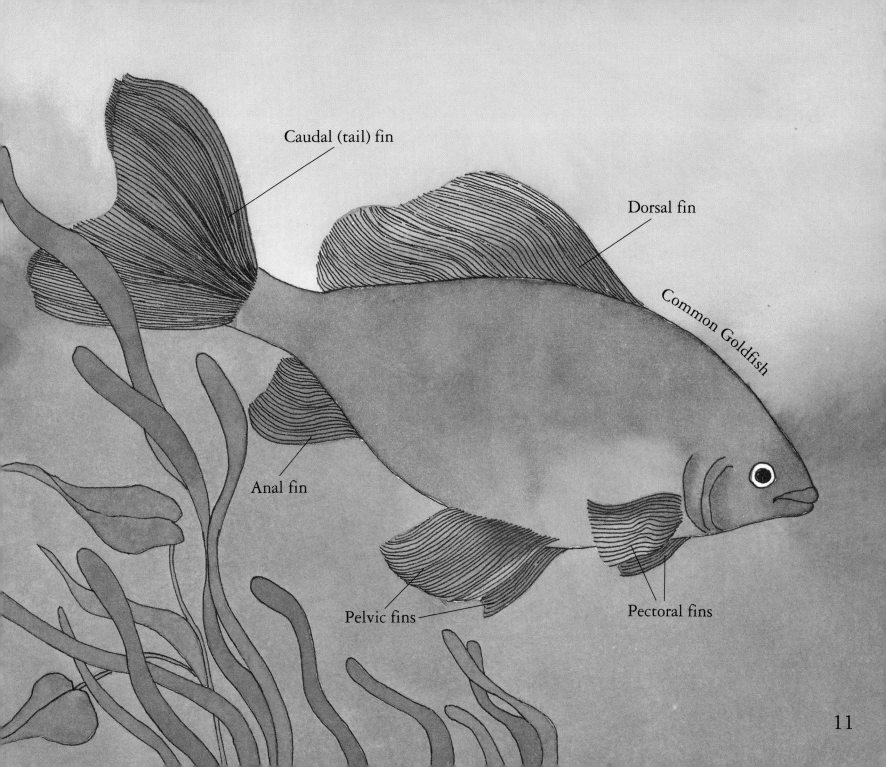

Caudal (tail) fin

Dorsal fin

Common Goldfish

Anal fin

Pelvic fins

Pectoral fins

11

Most fish have skin that is covered with scales. Scales help fish to swim too. The scales are hard and clear. They overlap like shingles on a roof. The smooth, slick scales let fish slide easily through the water.

A clear slime covers the scales. It helps fish glide through the water too.

Scales and slime also help to keep a fish healthy. The stiff scales protect a fish's delicate skin from cuts and scrapes. Many germs in the water get stuck in a fish's slime coating and are washed away before they can make the fish sick. Both scales and slime keep water from seeping into the fish's skin.

Arrowtail Goldfish

scales covered with slime

Common Shiner

13

When fish swim, they swing their tail fins back and forth and wave their other fins. They look as though they're flying through the water.

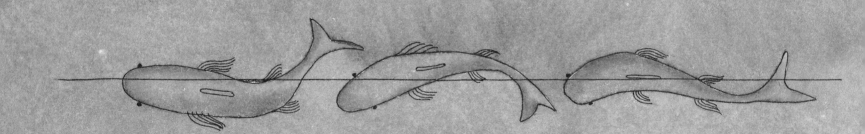

15

If you watch your goldfish, you'll see that they open and close their mouths. All day and all night. They look as if they're drinking water. But they're not. They're breathing.

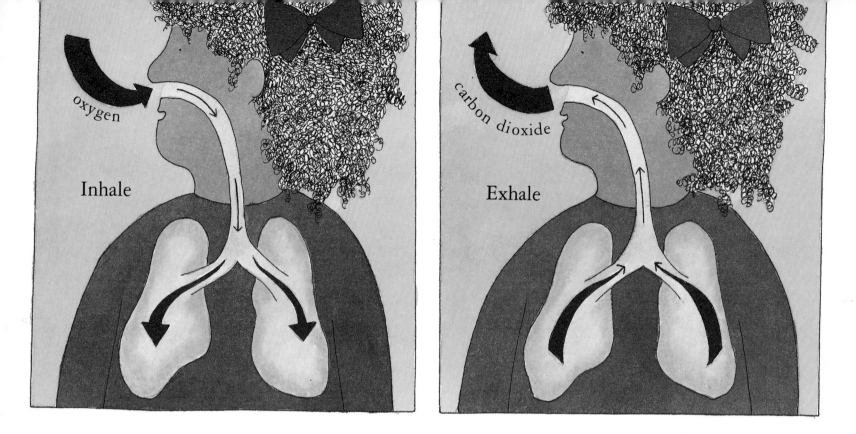

Inhale

oxygen

Exhale

carbon dioxide

You breathe all day and all night, too, but you can't breathe underwater the way fish do. Fish breathe with their gills. You breathe with your lungs.

You breathe in. Air goes to lungs inside your body. Your body takes the oxygen that you need from the air. Then you breathe out the parts of the air that you don't need.

Fish need oxygen too. There is oxygen in water, just as there is oxygen in air. A goldfish opens its mouth and lets some water in. When the fish closes its mouth, the water flows over the gills inside its body. The fish's body takes the oxygen it needs from the water. After passing over the gills, the water leaves the fish's body through gill openings. For a goldfish, opening and closing its mouth is just like breathing in and out.

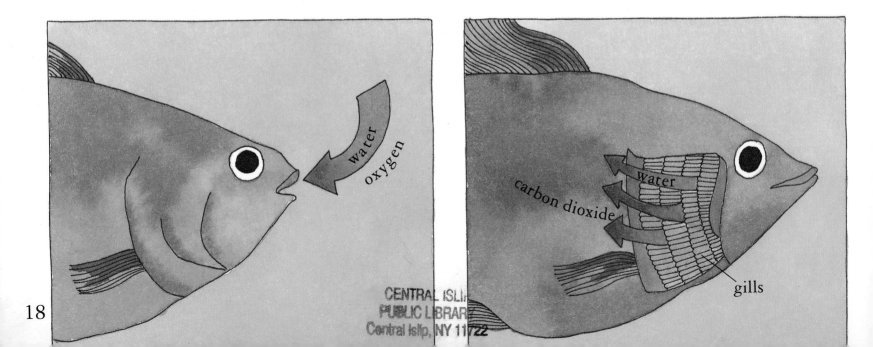

Comet

Black Goldfish

Veiltail

19

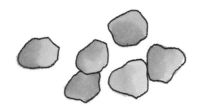

Fish need food just as you do, but they eat underwater. At feeding time, watch your goldfish flip their tails. They race to the top of the bowl, snap at their food, and gulp it down. They need only a tiny pinch of fish flakes each day. Good fish flakes are a mixture of ground-up flies, fish, shrimp, crab, oats, corn, carrots, and vitamins.

Veiltail

Albacore Tuna

Atlantic Mackerel

Striped Anchovy

22

Fish in the wild do not have someone to feed them
every day. Many fish eat tiny plants and animals so
small that you need a microscope to see them.
Bigger fish feed on worms, crabs, shrimp, and other
fish. Usually, big fish eat medium-sized fish, and
medium-sized fish eat small fish. This is part of
what we call the food chain.

Fish are cold-blooded. This means that their body temperature matches the temperature of the water around them. Be sure to place your goldfish bowl in a spot where the temperature will stay a steady 65 to 72 degrees Fahrenheit. This is the temperature fish need to be to stay healthy.

water's temperature 72°F

fish's temperature 72°F

You are warm-blooded. When you are healthy, your body temperature is about 98.6 degrees Fahrenheit. Your body stays this temperature by itself, whether the air around you is hot or cold.

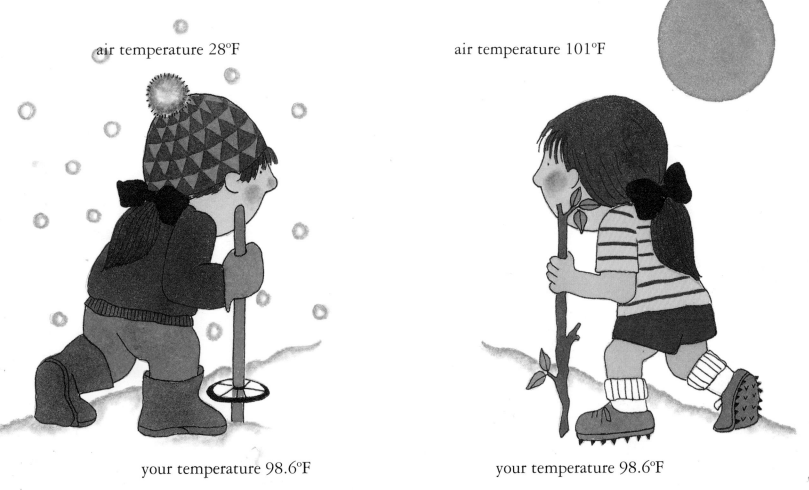

air temperature 28°F

air temperature 101°F

your temperature 98.6°F

your temperature 98.6°F

Sometimes goldfish swish their tails and zip around the bowl. Other times they look as if they've stopped moving, but they haven't. Their fins are always moving . . . even when they rest. Fish don't sleep as you do. They rest by moving very, very slowly.

Fishes' eyes are always open—they have no eyelids. So their eyes stay open even when they rest. Fish

Arrowtail

Calico

don't need eyelids, as you do, and they don't need tears, either. The water keeps their eyes washed. There is usually not enough light under water to bother fishes' eyes. Be sure not to put your goldfish in the sun, because it might be too bright for them.

Common Goldfish

Black Telescope Eye

28

With a sleek body, fins, scales, slime, and gills, a fish lives as naturally underwater as you do on land. Goldfish swim, breathe, eat, and rest in water. They slip over and under their castle, hide among water plants, and glide quietly around in their underwater world.

Setting Up a Goldfish Bowl

🐟 Start with a clean two-gallon fishbowl.

🐟 Wash some gravel by running water over it, and spread it over the bottom of the bowl.

🐟 Pour a few inches of cold water into the bowl.

🐟 Place some water plants firmly in the gravel and add a castle or some other decoration.

Gently pour in more water up to the widest part of the bowl—the more air surface, the more oxygen will be available for the fish.

 Let the water sit for a day to become room temperature.

 Now you can go to the pet store and get your goldfish.

 When you get home, float the plastic bag containing the goldfish in the bowl to let the fish get used to the water temperature.

 Wait 15 minutes.

 Open the bag. Let your goldfish swim out.

Your goldfish, like any pet, depends on you to take care of it. It's a good idea to study a fish care guide. That way you'll know just what to do to keep your goldfish healthy and happy.